Material Matters

Acids & Bases

EXPRESS EDITION

Carol Baldwin

Raintree

www.raintreepublishers.co.uk
Visit our website to find out more information about **Raintree** books.

To order:
☎ Phone 44 (0) 1865 888113
🗎 Send a fax to 44 (0) 1865 314091
🖥 Visit the Raintree Bookshop at **www.raintreepublishers.co.uk** to browse our catalogue and order online.

First published in Great Britain by Raintree Publishers, Halley Court, Jordan Hill, Oxford, OX2 8EJ, part of Harcourt Education Ltd.
Raintree is a registered trademark of Harcourt Education Ltd.

© Harcourt Education Ltd 2005
First published in paperback in 2005
The moral right of the proprietor has been asserted.

Produced for Raintree Publishers by Discovery Books Ltd.
Editorial: Louise Galpine, Carol Usher, Charlotte Guillain, and Isabel Thomas
Design: Victoria Bevan, Keith Williams (sprout.uk.com Limited), and Michelle Lisseter
Picture Research: Maria Joannou and Alison Prior
Production: Duncan Gilbert and Jonathan Smith
Originated by Dot Gradations Ltd
Printed and bound in China by South China Printing Company

ISBN 1 844 43382 X (hardback)
09 08 07 06 05
10 9 8 7 6 5 4 3 2 1

ISBN 1 844 43685 3 (paperback)
09 08 07 06 05
10 9 8 7 6 5 4 3 2 1

British Library Cataloguing in Publication Data
Baldwin, Carol, 1943–
Acids and bases – (Freestyle express. Material matters)
1. Acids – juvenile literature 2. Bases – (Chemistry)
–Juvenile literature
546.2'4

A full catalogue record for this book is available from the British Library.

This levelled text is a version of
Freestyle: Material Matters: Acids and Bases.

Photo acknowledgements
14–15, Andrew Lambert; 18–19, Art Directors & Trip; 13, Art Directors & Trip/A Lambert; 16 bott, Art Directors & Trip/G Hopkinson; 37 left, Art Directors & Trip/H Rogers; 12–13, Art Directors & Trip/R Chester; 30, Aspect/K Naylor; 40, Camera Press; 5 top, Camera Press/F Callanan; 7, Camera Press/F Callanan; 41, Camera Press/R Stonehouse; 19, Corbis; 24, Corbis; 31, Corbis; 34–35, Corbis; 40–41, all Corbis; 10–11, Corbis/A Nogues; 39, Corbis/G Diebold; 9, Corbis/Hulton Deutsch; 22–23, Corbis/K Fleming; 29, Corbis/W Blake; 16 right, Farmers weekly; 17 left, Farmers weekly; 32–33, Farmers weekly; 28–29, FLPA/B Borrell Casals; 4–5, FLPA/L West; 43, FLPA/L West; 18, FLPA/R Tidman; 20–21, FLPA/S Jonasson; 42–43, FLPA/W Wisniewski; 27, Mary Evans Picture Library; 20, NASA; 4, Oxford Scientific Films; 40–41, Photodisc; 16 left, Popperfoto/ Reuters/Juergen Schwartz; 15, Robert Harding Picture Library; 30–31, Robert Harding Picture Library/K Sherman; 5 bott, Robert Harding/K Sherman; 22, Science Photo Library; 23, Science Photo Library; 24–25, Science Photo Library; 25, Science Photo Library; 26–27, Science Photo Library; 35, Science Photo Library; 36, Science Photo Library; 38–39, Science Photo Library; 10, Science Photo Library/Andrew Lambert; 16 top, Science Photo Library/Garry Watson; 42, Science Photo Library/Josh Sher; 28, Shot in the Dark Cave Photography; 6, Trevor Clifford; 6–7, Trevor Clifford; 8, Trevor Clifford; 11, Trevor Clifford; 12, Trevor Clifford; 26, Trevor Clifford; 33, Trevor Clifford; 34, Trevor Clifford; 37 right, Trevor Clifford; 38, Trevor Clifford; 5 mid, 8–9, 14, 17 right, Tudor Photography.

Cover photograph of Linoleic acid crystals under a microscope reproduced with permission of Science Photo Library/ Eye Of Science.

Every effort has been made to contact copyright holders of any material reproduced in this book. Any omissions will be rectified in subsequent printings if notice is given to the Publishers.

Contents

Any words appearing in the text in bold, **like this**, are explained in the Glossary. You can also look out for some of them in the Word bank at the bottom of each page.

Outdoor attack

Stinging nettle

There are tiny barbs on the leaves and stems of stinging nettles. They can sting you when they rub against your skin. One of the chemicals that causes the pain is **formic acid**.

You are playing outside in the park. Something buzzes past your head. You swat it away. Ouch! A bee has stung you. When a bee stings you, it injects **venom**. Bee venom is an **acid**.

Acids are everywhere

Acids can be found everywhere. They taste sour. Lemon juice is sour; it contains **citric acid**. Vinegar contains **acetic acid**; it also has a sour taste. These acids are not dangerous; but some are. Some acids can burn you.

The chemical in a nettle sting is acid. Dock leaves contain a base. Rubbing dock leaves over the sting can help with the pain.

Word bank acid compound that tastes sour and may burn you. It contains hydrogen and has a pH less than 7.

Bases are in places you might not expect

Bases can be found all over the home. Bases have a bitter taste. They also feel slippery. Soap is a base. Baking soda is another base you might have in your home. These bases will not harm you. But some bases can burn your skin.

A base is a **chemical** that can cancel out an acid.

The venom of a wasp contains a base. So an acid, like vinegar, can help with the pain.

Find out later...

... why our muscles can get sore.

... why water in a swimming pool needs to be tested.

... why these trees are dying.

base compound that tastes bitter and feels slippery. It has a pH of more than 7.

Acids and bases

Storing acidic foods

Some foods, like pickles, are **preserved** in weak acids. They should not be stored in aluminium foil. The acids can eat holes in the foil. That is why these pickled gherkins are stored in a glass jar.

Weak acids, like vinegar, stop **bacteria** growing.

All **acids** share certain **properties**. Acids taste sour. Foods like yogurt, pickles, and grapefruit all taste sour. They all contain acids. But it is not safe to test if something is an acid by tasting it. Some acids are very **toxic**, like the liquid inside a car battery.

The best way to test whether something is an acid is to use a **chemical** called an **indicator**. Acids **react** with indicators to produce colour changes.

Word bank   preserve stop something from going rotten

Common acids

Acids are found in many things.
You come across them everyday:

- fizzy drinks contain carbonic acid
- apples contain malic acid
- your stomach contains hydrochloric acid
- sour milk contains lactic acid.

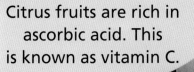

Citrus fruits are rich in ascorbic acid. This is known as vitamin C.

Muscle acids

This sprinter is running very fast. Her muscles need extra energy. This comes from a **chemical reaction** in her muscle **cells**. Lactic acid is also produced. Too much lactic acid will make her muscles ache.

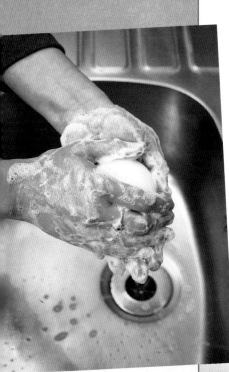

What are bases like?

Bases taste bitter and feel slippery. Soap and **detergents**, like washing-up liquid, are bases. Some bases, like drain cleaner and oven cleaner will burn you. It is not safe to test if a **chemical** is a base by taste or touch.

You can use chemicals, called **indicators**, to test if something is a base. When an indicator, called litmus, **reacts** with a base, its colour changes to blue.

Slippery soap

Have you ever dropped a bar of wet soap in the shower? Sometimes soap just slips out of your hand. This is because soap is a base and bases are slippery.

Many household products, like these soaps, creams, and foams, contain bases.

Word bank detergent liquid used with water to remove dirt

Bases around us

Many household products contain bases:

- deodorants
- medicines used to treat upset stomachs
- building materials, like mortar and plaster.

Not many foods contain bases. But bases are found in egg whites, cooked lobster and shrimp, and baking soda.

Bases are used to make **dyes**, medicines, and cloth.

Lime pits

When London was bombed in World War II many people died. The bodies were buried in pits filled with calcium oxide. This is called **lime**. Lime destroys flesh. This helped prevent disease spreading.

Bases in water

Bases are **compounds**. This means they are made from two or more **elements** joined together. Elements are made from only one type of **atom** or tiny particle.

Many bases are **hydroxide** compounds. This means they contain a hydrogen and an oxygen atom.

Most bases **dissolve** in water. Those that do this are called **alkalis**. Alkalis can **conduct** electricity.

Ammonia fountain

Ammonia gas in the top flask **reacts** with water. This forms ammonium hydroxide. This is an alkali. That is why the **universal indicator** has turned violet.

This is an ammonia fountain. Ask your teacher to set this up in your class.

element material made from only one type of atom or tiny particle that makes up everything

Acids in water

Acids are a group of compounds that all contain hydrogen. When an acid dissolves in water it splits apart. The hydrogen becomes free. It carries an electric charge. This means acids can conduct electricity.

Car batteries make use of this **property**. They contain two plates made from different metals. The plates are connected together and placed in sulphuric acid. The acid conducts the electricity.

Lemon battery

A lemon can make electricity. The metal wires are connected to the inside of a lemon. The lemon's acid conducts electricity.

People must be careful when they throw away old car batteries. The sulphuric acid in them can burn skin.

The reading on the meter shows that a small amount of electricity is flowing.

conduct allow electricity to pass through easily

Indicators and pH

Litmus colours

Remember the colour that litmus paper turns in acids and bases this way:

- An aciD turns litmus reD.
- A basE turns litmus bluE.

In each case, both words end in the same letter.

The **pH scale** shows if something is **acidic** or **basic**. It goes from 0 to 14. If a material has a pH of less than 7 it is an **acid**. If a material has a pH of more than 7, it is a **base**. A material with a pH of 7 is **neutral**. It is neither acidic or basic.

Indicators

An **indicator** is a **chemical** that changes colour when the pH changes. It is used to find out if a **solution** is acidic, basic, or neutral.

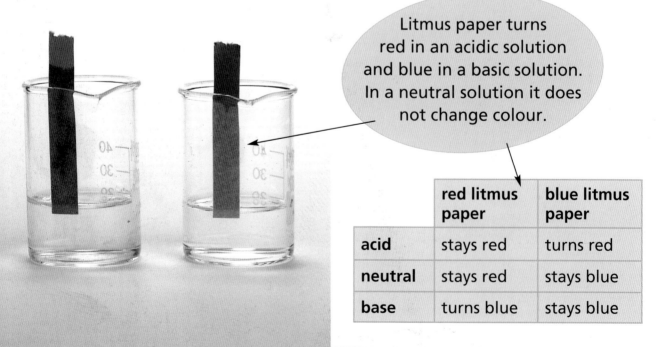

Litmus paper turns red in an acidic solution and blue in a basic solution. In a neutral solution it does not change colour.

	red litmus paper	blue litmus paper
acid	stays red	turns red
neutral	stays red	stays blue
base	turns blue	stays blue

pH scale numbers from 0 to 14 used to show the strengths of acids and bases

Litmus

Litmus can test for an acid or a base. It comes in the form of paper or a solution.

There are other indicators that can tell us more about pH:

- Methyl orange can show if an acid is strong. It changes from red to orange.
- Alazarin yellow changes from yellow to red. It can tell you if a base is strong or weak.

pH meters

You can measure the pH of a solution with a pH meter. This measures the pH exactly. A probe is put in the solution and the pH reading appears on a dial.

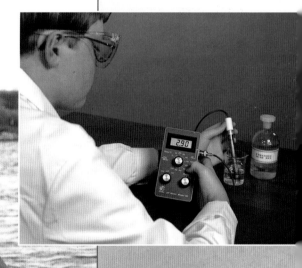

Scientists can use battery-operated pH meters outdoors.

neutral neither acidic nor basic, with a pH of 7

Swimming pool chemistry

A chlorine **compound** is added to swimming pools. This is an acid. If the water in swimming pools gets too acidic it stings your eyes. The acidity of pool water is checked every day in case this happens.

Universal indicator

Universal indicator is a special indicator. It will show colour changes for the whole **pH scale** — from pH 0–14. It shows how **acidic** or **basic** a **solution** is. Universal indicator comes in paper or liquid form. If you add some liquid universal indicator to a solution or dip the paper in, it changes colour. You can match the colour to a chart. This will tell you the pH of the solution you are testing.

The colours of universal indicator are like the colours of the rainbow. Strong acids turn universal indicator red, and strong bases turn it violet.

The water in a swimming pool should be about pH 7.5.

0   1   2   3   4   5   6

Word bank   solution solid dissolved in a liquid

Natural indicators

Many plant **extracts** can tell us the pH of a material. Tea is a natural indicator. An **acid**, like lemon juice will turn tea pale yellow. A **base**, such as sodium bicarbonate, will turn tea dark brown. Why not try this yourself?

Juice from red cabbages is bluish-purple in a **neutral** liquid. But in a strong acid it turns red and in a weak acid it changes to purple. It turns greenish in a weak base and yellow in a strong base.

Flower power
Hydrangeas, like these, act as natural indicators. The flowers are pink if the hydrangea is growing on basic soil. The flowers are blue if the plant is growing on acidic soil.

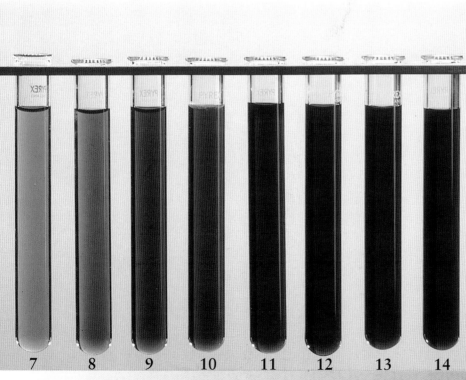

7   8   9   10   11   12   13   14

extract something that is taken from a material

Neutralization reactions

When an **acid** and a **base react** together they cancel each other out. The solution left after the reaction is **neutral**. It has neither acid nor base **properties**. This is called a **neutralization** reaction.

When an acid and a base react, water and a **salt** are always formed.

Bases to the rescue

Acid fires, like the one below, or spills can be very dangerous. The fire crew is blowing a base over the acid. The base **neutralizes** the acid.

If the soil is too acidic farmers can use **lime**. This neutralizes the soil.

neutralization reaction between an acid and a base to form a salt and water

Salts

A salt is any **compound**, other than water, formed from a neutralization reaction. The metal from the base gives a salt the first part of its name. The non-metal from the acid forms the second part. In the example below <u>calcium</u> is the metal from the base. The <u>sulphate</u> comes from the sulphuric acid. This forms the salt, calcium sulphate.

Acid	Base	Salt formed
Sulphuric acid H_2SO_4	Calcium hydroxide $Ca(OH)_2$	Calcium sulphate $CaSO_4$

This example shows the salt formed when this acid and base pair react.

If the water in a swimming pool is more than pH 7.6 **bacteria** will grow.

More swimming pool chemistry

Water in a swimming pool has to be above pH 7.4 or it will be too **acidic**. If it falls below this a weak base is added. This neutralizes the acid and raises the pH.

More about salts

Salts are among the most important **chemicals** in the world. The most common salt is sodium chloride, or table salt. It has thousands of uses. Farmers use salt for **cattle licks**. Meat packers **preserve** meats with salt. Salt is used to treat leather, for making glass, and other chemicals.

There are many other important salts. Potassium nitrate is just one of them. It is used to make explosives and **fertilizers**.

Heaps of salt

Much of the salt we use comes from seawater. The water **evaporates** and leaves the salt behind. It is collected at special salt works.

This woman is restoring an old book. She is applying a weak base to the pages. This neutralizes the acid in the paper.

fertilizer chemical that gives plants the elements they need for healthy growth

Saving old books

When books become old, their pages break easily and crumble away. This is because the paper in the books becomes **acidic** over time. Libraries want to save their books. So they use a process to **neutralize** the **acid**. This involves soaking the book in a weak **base**. Some of the base stays in the pages and protects them for many more years.

This map of the stars is an historic document. It would crumble if acid in the paper is not neutralized.

Book bath
The books are placed in a weak base, so the liquid can reach all the pages. After about 25 minutes, the liquid is sucked out. In two hours the books are dry.

evaporate change from a liquid to a gas

More about acids

Sulphuric acid

Sulphur is a yellow solid. Sulphur is burned to produce sulphur dioxide gas. Sulphuric **acid** is made from sulphur dioxide.

Pure sulphuric acid is a colourless, oily liquid. Sulphuric acid is used to make **fertilizers**, **dyes**, paper, and materials like **rayon**.

Acid rain!

High above the planet Venus is a thick layer of clouds. They are made of tiny droplets of sulphuric acid.

Word bank   dye chemical used to change the colour of something

Properties of sulphuric acid

Sulphuric acid can remove water from materials. These reactions produce lots of heat. Sulphuric acid causes terrible burns because it removes water from the skin.

What happens when sulphuric acid is poured on to sugar? It foams and starts to steam. All the water **evaporates** off in the heat. Only a black lump of carbon is left.

Sulphuric acid

Sulphuric acid is the acid we use most. This pie chart shows how it is used.

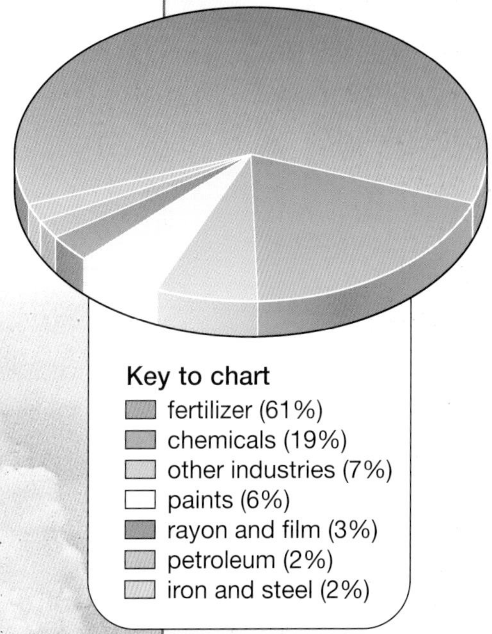

Key to chart
- fertilizer (61%)
- chemicals (19%)
- other industries (7%)
- paints (6%)
- rayon and film (3%)
- petroleum (2%)
- iron and steel (2%)

Volcanoes produce large amounts of sulphur dioxide gas. This dissolves in water to form sulphuric acid.

rayon cloth used to make lightweight clothing

Phosphoric acid

Phosphoric acid is used to make **fertilizers** and phosphates. Phosphates are added to washing powders. They help the washing powder clean better.

But phosphates can get into streams and lakes. Then they cause **pollution**.

Royal water

Royal water is a mixture of nitric acid and hydrochloric acid. It can separate gold from silver. It **dissolves** the gold and leaves the silver behind.

Nitric acid

Nitric acid is used to make fertilizers and explosives. It is also used in plastics, such as nylon. Jackets and parachutes are made from nylon.

pollution harmful things in the air, water, or land

Hydrochloric acid

Large amounts of hydrochloric acid are used by the steel industry. It cleans the surface of iron and steel.

Hydrochloric acid is also used to clean stone buildings and swimming pools.

We have hydrochloric acid in our stomachs. It helps to break down foods like meat, fish, and eggs. These foods contain a lot of **protein**. When our stomachs become too **acidic** we get upset stomachs.

Fizzing rocks

When limestone is dropped into hydrochloric acid, it gives off bubbles. This is carbon dioxide gas. This happens with marble and chalk too.

Dynamite is used in mining and tunnel building. It is made from nitric acid.

protein compound needed by the body for growth and repair

Etching glass

Etching is when people write or make images on glass. They do this by using **acid**. They coat the glass with wax. A design is drawn in the wax with a sharp needle. The glass is then dipped in hydrofluoric acid. The acid eats away the glass that is not covered by wax. This makes a design.

Storing hydrofluoric acid

Hydrofluoric acid cannot be stored in glass bottles; it 'eats through' glass. It is stored in plastic bottles.

> These glass objects have been etched using acid.

> This light bulb is made out of 'frosted' glass. The glass has been dipped into hydrofluoric acid to remove its smooth surface.

Word bank   etching design made when an acid eats into glass or metal

Old newspapers and books

Paper is usually made from wood. Wood chips are treated with **chemicals** to break them down into **wood pulp**. This makes **wood pulp** very **acidic**.

Wood contains **lignin**. Lignin is a substance that keeps wood stiff. Lignin breaks down over time and becomes acidic too.

How long a book lasts depends on how acidic the paper is and how much lignin it contains. Some wood pulp has most of the lignin removed. Paper made from this will last a long time.

Spray away
Ants make **formic acid** in their bodies. They use the acid to bite and sting. People first got formic acid by crushing ants.

This red wood ant sprays acid at its enemies.

lignin gummy material that makes wood stiff

Acids and metals

Acids react with some metals, such as calcium, aluminium, and zinc. But acids do not react with all metals. For example, platinum and silver do not react with acids. When an acid reacts with a metal, the metal disappears and there is lots of fizzing. The reaction produces a **salt** and hydrogen gas.

One way to make salts is to react acids with metals.

Skin care

Epsom salts are used to heal some skin rashes. They contain magnesium sulphate.

Epsom salts are formed when sulphuric acid reacts with the **base**, magnesium **hydroxide**.

Word bank crystal solid with particles arranged in a regular, repeated pattern

Making etchings

For hundreds of years acids and metal plates have been used to make **etchings**. A metal plate is coated with a thin layer of wax. The artist draws in the wax. This uncovers parts of the metal. The plate is dipped in the acid. The acid reacts with the uncovered metal. Ink is forced into the etched areas of the plate with a roller. Paper is pressed on to the inked surface and a print of an etching is made.

Wide or thin lines

Printmakers use different acids on the metal plates. Nitric acid is used to make thick lines.

This photo shows a **magnified** salt **crystal**.

The metal plates used to make etchings like this could be copper, zinc, or iron.

Acids and carbonates

Acids **react** with **carbonates**. A **salt**, water, and carbon dioxide gas are produced. Caves form when **acidic** water reacts with carbonate rocks. Limestone, chalk, and marble are all types of carbonate rocks.

How caves form

Rainwater joins with carbon dioxide in the air. This makes weak carbonic acid. This acid reacts with calcium carbonate rocks, like limestone. Caves and tunnels are made as the acid eats through the rock.

Lechuguilla Cave

This cave is in New Mexico. It formed when sulphuric acid ate through the limestone underground.

Lechuguilla Cave is an exciting place to explore.

stalactite

column cave formation made when stalactites and stalagmites join up

Cave features

In a cave there is water on the surface of the rocks. This water contains a lot of calcium carbonate. As the water drips and **evaporates** it leaves solid calcium carbonate behind.

The calcium carbonate forms wonderful shapes over time. When water drips from the cave's roof, **stalactites** form. They hang down like icicles. As water drips on to the floor, towers form. These are called **stalagmites**.

The Big Room is in Carlsbad **Caverns**, New Mexico. It is larger than four football fields. Its ceiling is high enough to hold a 22-storey building.

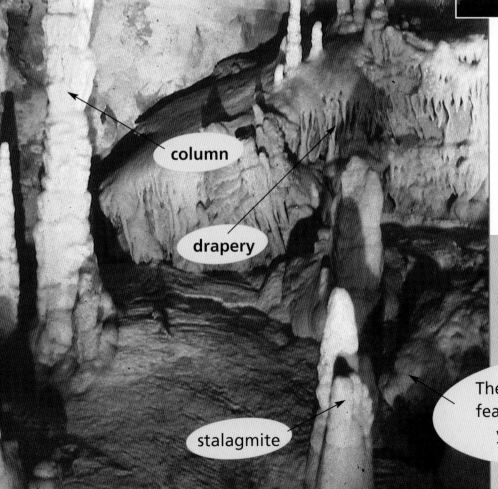

column

drapery

stalagmite

These kinds of cave features take many years to form.

drapery cave formation that forms in folds

Liming

This is Borsjan Lake in Norway. It was once dead because the water was so acidic. **Lime** or calcium **hydroxide** was added to **neutralize** the water.

Acid rain

Coal, gas, and oil are **fossil fuels**. When fossil fuels are burned, sulphur dioxide and nitrogen **oxide** gases are produced. In the air, these gases join with water. This reaction forms sulphuric acid and nitric acid. The acids fall to the Earth in rain and snow.

Acid rain reacts with marble and limestone. This ruins many buildings and statues. It also makes soils **acidic** and some plants cannot grow in them.

Borsjan Lake is now full of plants and animals.

fossil fuel fuel formed from the remains of plants and animals that lived millions of years ago; coal, gas, and oil are fossil fuels

Reducing acid rain

It is not easy to reduce acid rain. We can use less fuel. We also need to stop the sulphur dioxide and nitrogen oxides getting into the air. Power plants can use coal with less sulphur or with the sulphur removed.

Car engines burn petrol or diesel fuel. This produces nitrogen oxides. Cars now have **catalytic converters** in their exhausts. These break down nitrogen oxides into less harmful gases.

What can you do?

Using less electricity and petrol reduces acid rain. You can help:

- turn off lights and computers when you are not using them

- only use electric appliances when you have to

- use public transport, walk, or ride a bicycle whenever you can.

Acid rain fell on these spruce trees. Now the trees are dead.

Ride a bike. It will help to reduce acid rain!

catalytic converter device that removes chemicals from exhaust fumes

More about bases

Sodium hydroxide

Sodium **hydroxide** is a very strong **base**.
Its common name is caustic soda. It is very
dangerous. Sodium hydroxide attacks metals
and it burns or destroys flesh. Many **chemicals**
catch fire or explode when they come into
contact with sodium hydroxide.

Sodium hydroxide breaks down oil and grease.
So **dilute** sodium hydroxide is used to clean
drains and ovens. In industry it is used to make
other chemicals, paper, soap, glass, and **rayon**.

Moving sodium hydroxide

Sodium hydroxide
is carried in tankers.
On the side of
the tanker you
will find this
information plate.
The number tells
us what the
chemical is.

DANGER
Corrosion risk

You will find
this warning sign on the
containers of strong acids and
bases. It tells us how
dangerous they are.

Word bank   dilute having a small amount of material dissolved in water

This ammonium nitrate will be used as a fertilizer.

Ammonia

Ammonia is used a lot. Pure ammonia gas has no colour and a sharp smell. Too much of this gas can kill. Ammonia gas **dissolves** in water and forms ammonium hydroxide. This is good for cleaning. Many cleaning products contain ammonia. You can tell if they do by their smell.

Ammonia is used to make many chemicals. One of these is nitric **acid**. It is also used in **fertilizers** and to make rayon and nylon. Ammonium nitrate is made by reacting ammonia with nitric acid. This is used in fertilizers and explosives.

17 mls

Smelling Salts

ANTI-CATARRH

CLEARS AND RELIEVES

Smelling salts
Smelling salts may be put under someone's nose when they faint. Smelling salts give off ammonia. Ammonia helps a person to breathe faster. Then they should come round.

dissolve mix completely and evenly

Soap making

Soap is made when fats or oils **react** with a **base**. In the past people used to make their own soap. They used animal fats and the ashes from wood fires. Wood ashes contain the base potassium **hydroxide**. To make hard soap **salt** was added.

When the mixture had set, the bars were allowed to air for a few weeks. This was done so that any leftover base would be **neutralized**. Otherwise the soap would burn the skin.

Hand lotion puts oils back into the skin.

Dry hands

The bases in soap react with oil in your skin, as well as with dirt. If you wash your hands often, the soap can take out too much oil. Then your skin becomes rough and dry.

neutralize make neutral, so material is not an acid or a base

How soap works

Soap helps water to stick to things better. Water has a sort of skin. This is called **surface tension**. This skin has to be broken for something to get wet. Soap breaks the surface tension and things can get wet.

Dirt collects in the grease on skin and clothes. Soap grabs the grease and takes it into the water. This leaves skin or clothes squeaky clean.

Soap scum

Hard water has calcium or magnesium salts **dissolved** in it. These salts react with soap. Waxy solids are formed. They are called soap scum.

Today, soap is made in factories. Many soaps have perfumes and colour added to them.

Soap scum sticks on to the sides of the sink.

---

surface tension force that pulls the particles of a liquid together at its surface

Strength of acids and bases

Tooth decay
Bacteria in our mouths make acids from sugary foods. These acids are weak, but they still dissolve **minerals** in our teeth. These acids can make holes in our teeth.

All **acids** share certain **properties**. But not all acids are alike. Some are safe to swallow; others will cause serious burns. This is because some acids are stronger than others. This is true of **bases** as well.

Sulphuric acid is a strong acid. A weak acid is **acetic acid**. This is found in vinegar. A strong base is sodium **hydroxide**. It is very dangerous. A weak base is ammonium hydroxide.

The black part of this X-ray is a hole. It is caused by weak acids in the mouth. Brushing your teeth after a sugary snack helps to dilute the acids.

Word bank   **mineral** non-living compound found in nature that is solid

Concentration

A strong acid or base is not the same thing as a **concentrated** acid or base. A concentrated acid has a lot of acid **dissolved** in water. A **diluted** acid has only a small amount of acid dissolved in water.

Lemons taste more sour than oranges do. This is because there is more **citric acid** in lemons than there is in oranges. The citric acid in lemon juice is more concentrated than in orange juice.

Drinks

Sometimes drinks are sold in concentrated form. Before you drink them, you have to dilute them with water.

This drink is dilute. Only a small amount of drink concentrate has been added to the water.

concentrated having a large amount of material dissolved in a small volume of water

Fizzy drinks

Bubbles of carbon dioxide are added to drinks to make them fizzy. The carbon dioxide gas **dissolves** in the drink. This makes fizzy drinks **acidic**. They are bad for your teeth.

The end point

You can see how strong an **acid** or a **base** is by **neutralizing** it. Measure the **dilute** acid into a beaker. Add a few drops of an **indicator** called phenolphthalein (say "feen-ul-thayl-een"). Then, add a weak base one drop at a time. Count the number of drops. When the indicator turns bright pink, the acid is neutralized. This is the **end point**. You can tell how strong an acid is by how many drops of base are needed to neutralize it.

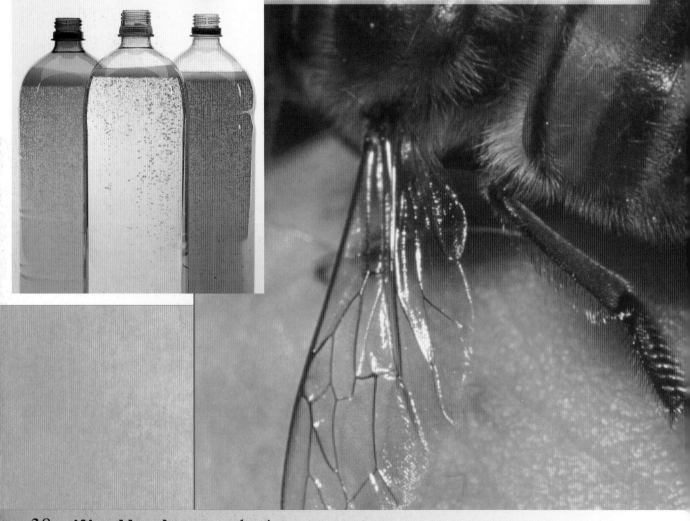

Word bank   end point point at which an acid and a base have reacted completely

An upset stomach

At some time, most of us have had a stomach ache. Usually too much acid in our stomachs causes the pain. If you take an **antacid**, it helps you feel better.

Antacids are medicines. They contain small amounts of a weak base. The weak base neutralizes the extra acid in the stomach.

Antacids often contain aluminium **hydroxide**. This reacts with the hydrochloric acid in the stomach. Water and aluminium chloride are formed.

Antacids
Antacids often come in tablets that you add to a glass of water. The antacid below could contain calcium hydroxide.

Baking soda is a weak base. It will neutralize the acid in a bee's sting. Vinegar is a weak acid. It neutralizes the base in a wasp's sting.

Measuring pH

The **pH scale** tells us how **acidic** or **alkaline** a solution is, or if it is **neutral**. A strong **acid** has a low pH. A strong **base** has a high pH. A material with a pH of 7 is neither an acid nor a base. It is **neutral**.

Strong acids, like hydrochloric acid, have a pH near 0. Weak acids, such as **citric acid**, have a pH between 2 and 5. Tomato juice contains citric acid. It has a pH of about 4.

Acids, such as vinegar, can **preserve** food.

Safe pickles

You can make pickles at home. But you have to be careful. The pH of pickles should be below 3. If the pH is higher, **bacteria** will grow and make **toxins**. The toxins can cause food poisoning.

0   1   2   3   4   5   6

A strong base has a pH near 14. Sodium **hydroxide** is a strong base. It has a pH of 14. The pH of a weak base would be between 9 and 12. Ammonia **solution** is a weak base. It has a pH of about 11.

Water has a pH of 7. If you add water to an acid, the **diluted** acid will have a slightly higher pH. If you dilute a base it will lower the pH a little.

Skin and hair have a pH of between 5 and 6. A shampoo that is pH-balanced has a pH close to the pH of our skin and hair.

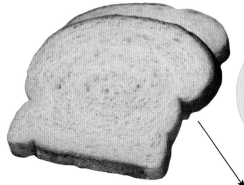

Here are some items of food and drink. The arrows show their pH on the scale.

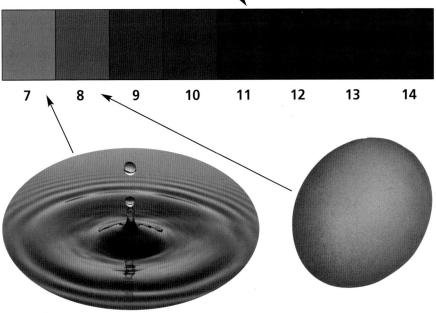

| 7 | 8 | 9 | 10 | 11 | 12 | 13 | 14 |

dilute having a small amount of substance dissolved in water

The pH of blood

Blood is pumped around the body. It carries oxygen and food to **cells**. It takes away carbon dioxide and other waste products. The pH of blood cannot change much or it will not work properly.

Compounds called **buffers** help to keep the pH of blood the same. They react with any added **acids** or **bases**.

Sometimes the blood pH changes too much for the buffers to cope. Then the blood pH becomes too high or too low. This can damage the body's organs, like the kidneys or liver.

Testing blood pH

Some diseases, like diabetes and asthma, change the blood's pH. People with diseases like these have their blood pH tested from time to time.

Plants like cacti grow well in basic desert soils.

buffer material that reduces the change in pH that happens when an acid or base is added to a solution

The pH of soils

Soils can be between about pH 3 and 10. Acid soils are found in wet areas. Dead plants rot easily when the soil is wet. Rotting plants make the soil more **acidic**.

Evergreen trees, such as pine and spruce, grow well in acidic soil. But they will die if the soil is too acidic.

Minerals that contain calcium or magnesium make soil **basic**. Very basic soils are usually found in deserts. There is hardly any rain to wash the minerals away. There are also few plants to rot and add acids to the soil.

Clearing forests for farming

The soil in an evergreen forest is acidic. Most food crops grow best in more **neutral** soil. So, cutting down evergreen forests to grow food is not a good idea.

These are blueberries. They grow well in acidic soil.

Find out more

Websites
BBC Science
News, features, and activities on science.
www.bbc.co.uk

Creative Chemistry
Fun, practical activities, quizzes, puzzles, and more.
www.creative-chemistry.org.uk

skoool.co.uk
Help with science projects and homework.
http://kent.skoool.co.uk

Books
Chemicals in Action: Acids and Bases, Ann Fullick (Heinemann Library, 2000)
Material Matters: Chemical Reactions, Carol Baldwin (Raintree, 2005)
Materials All Around Us, Robert Snedden (Heinemann Library, 2001)

World Wide Web
To find out more about acids and bases you can search the Internet. Use keywords like these:

- "acid rain"
- acids +bases
- "blood pH"

You can find your own keywords by using words from this book. The search tips opposite will help you find useful websites.

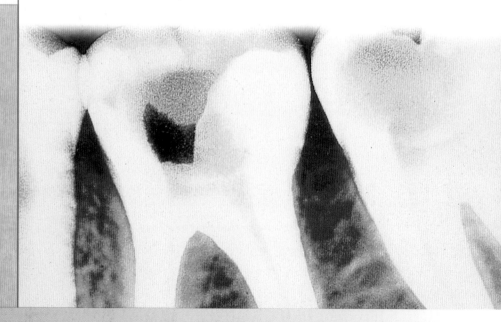

Search tips

There are billions of pages on the Internet. It can be difficult to find exactly what you are looking for. These tips will help you find useful websites more quickly:

- know what you want to find out about
- use simple keywords
- use two to six keywords in a search
- only use names of people, places or things
- put quote marks around words that go together, for example "acid rain"

Where to search

Search engine

A search engine looks through millions of website pages. It lists all the sites that match the words in the search box. You will find the best matches are at the top of the list, on the first page.

Search directory

A person instead of a computer has sorted a search directory. You can search by keyword or subject and browse through the different sites. It is like looking through books on a library shelf.

Glossary

acetic acid acid found in vinegar

acid compound that tastes sour and may burn you. It contains hydrogen and has a pH less than 7.

acid rain rain that contains sulphuric acid and nitric acid

acidic containing an acid

alkali base that will dissolve in water

antacid medicine used to treat an upset stomach

atom tiny particle that makes up everything

bacteria tiny living things, which can cause disease

base compound that tastes bitter and feels slippery. It has a pH of more than 7.

basic containing a base

buffer material that reduces the change in pH that happens when an acid or base is added to a solution

carbonate compound containing a metal plus carbon and oxygen

catalytic converter device that removes chemicals from exhaust fumes

cattle lick block of salt and minerals that cattle can lick to make sure they have enough minerals in their diet

cavern very large cave

cell building block that makes up all living things

chemical any material made by or used in chemistry

chemical reaction change that produces one or more new materials

citric acid acid found in lemons, limes, and oranges

column cave formation made when stalactites and stalagmites join up

compound material made of two or more elements joined together. Water is a compound of oxygen and hydrogen.

concentrated having a large amount of material dissolved in a small volume of water

conduct allow electricity to pass through easily

crystal solid with particles arranged in a regular, repeated pattern

detergent liquid used with water to remove dirt

dilute having a small amount of material dissolved in water

dissolve mix completely and evenly

drapery cave formation that forms in folds

dye chemical used to change the colour of something

element material made from only one type of atom or tiny particle that makes up everything

end point point at which an acid and a base have reacted completely

etching design made when an acid eats into glass or metal

evaporate change from a liquid to a gas

evergreen plants that do not lose their leaves in winter

extract something that is taken from a material

fertilizer chemical that gives plants the elements they need for healthy growth

formic acid acid found in the bodies of ants and some plants

fossil fuel fuel formed from the remains of plants and animals that lived millions of years ago. Coal, gas, and oil are fossil fuels.

hydroxide compound containing a metal, hydrogen, and oxygen

indicator chemical that changes colour in acids and bases

lignin gummy material that makes wood stiff

lime calcium hydroxide or calcium oxide

magnified made to look bigger

mineral non-living compound found in nature that is solid

neutral neither acidic nor basic, with a pH of 7

neutralization reaction between an acid and a base to form a salt and water

neutralize make neutral, so material is not an acid or a base

oxide compound of oxygen and another element

pH scale numbers from 0 to 14 used to show the strengths of acids and bases

pollution harmful things in the air, water, or land

preserve stop something from going rotten

property feature of something

protein compound needed by the body for growth and repair

rayon cloth used to make lightweight clothing

react take part in a chemical reaction

salt compound formed from a reaction between an acid and base

solution solid dissolved in a liquid

stalactite icicle-like formation that hangs from the roof of a cave

stalagmite cone-shaped formation that forms from the floor of a cave

surface tension force that pulls the particles of a liquid together at its surface

toxic can harm or kill you, like a poison

toxin material that is poisonous

universal indicator paper or liquid indicator that shows colour changes for the whole pH scale

venom poison injected by biting or stinging

wood pulp ground-up wood mixed with chemicals

Index